The Saccharine Abstraction of Everything

Anagha Ratish

INDIA • SINGAPORE • MALAYSIA

*To my best friends, my psych ward, for whom
I have written many of these poems.*

Contents

A Postscript (Or Preface, Depending on How You Look at It) from my Future Self

I was fourteen when I wrote much of this,

A little older for the latter bit.

As I write this, I am all of sixteen.

Already, I find myself with changed views and am tempted to do away with half of what I have written.

But I cannot, for that would be a disservice to my younger self.

I have merely moved things around, so that this becomes a reminiscence of the future, a prediction of the past.

And so, this volume is a mishmash;

Of the words in my mind,

me now,

me then,

And sometimes me tomorrow.

An Utterly Uninspiring Notebook

The girl sits; not in front of a window, or watching a sunset, or doing anything remotely interesting. She simply sits, and she is filled with a nervous energy. Her fingers drum the table, matching the rapid tempo of her heart. There are words in her mind, but she cannot feel the shape of them. So, she sits at her table, and opens a notebook. It isn't a leather-bound notebook, weathered and ancient, or even a new notebook. It is only something left over from school, halfway filled with more sketches than notes.

And there she writes.

There, she tries to learn the shape of her words again.

The Beginning (Again)

Where do I begin?
It would help
If only I knew
What I am trying to say.

What has changed?
The sky? The stars,
The colour of the trees?
No. Just me.

This time,
There is no beginning
And no end,
For this is not a story.

This is an attempt,
To dissect the overlapping
Shards and sections
Of my mind.

An attempt,
To untangle the snarled
Yarn and thread of my thoughts,
Fraying but dizzyingly vibrant.

I do not know where this begins.

Or where it ends

Or where it goes

Or even what it is

For I don't even know

my

own

mind.

The One in the Mirror

The girl looks in the mirror.

She's been staring at herself for a while now.

But it's not vanity that inspires her.

She has eyes, like many do, and they happen to be brown.

A nose, perfectly ordinary.

Lips, always bitten raw.

Hair, framing her face like a cloud.

But who is she, beyond her face, beyond the things that she can see?

Who is she?

Me (If Such A Thing Exists)

Who

am

I?

Once before,

I have questioned this.

Two years later,

I still

do

not

know.

How many times,

I wonder;

How many poems will it take to

figure

it

out?

I study myself in the mirror,

Two eyes, not blue, green, or grey

But the most ordinary shade of brown there could be,

Lined perpetually with smudged kohl,

A nose in the centre, usual as can be;

Lips, ears ornamented with dangling earrings,

Hair, glasses pink as bubblegum;

But what is

The shape

The size

The colour

of

my

soul?

I know my name.

I know my face.

I know my age,

And a little of what I like

And dislike.

But who

Do these

features

belong

to?

What shall I say

When someone asks me

Who I am?

My name?

Is that my only identification?

Fourteen and already confronted
With the truths
of
my
identity.

I am haunted by the ghosts of my selves.
A matryoshka doll,
The versions of myself
Stacked, each only slightly different;
Each believing itself better
than
the
last.

My blue hair,
My glasses, nearly
too big for my face
My jewellery;
Who do people
think
I
am?

(Already, I worry that I am too presumptuous in
assuming that people think of me at all.)

Once again,

I wonder

How can I be a single person

When there are so many facets of me?

Of merely how

people

perceive

me?

Is there no such thing

As "myself"

At all?

How can there be

When there are

so

many

mes?

The me I am.

The me I think I am.

The me I pretend to be.

And the me that people see.

And even my words

May not be my own;

Maybe all of these thoughts,

These sentences,

Are things I've read and heard,

Been taught;

Mishmashes of

Other people's minds.

So perhaps

Even that part of me

Doesn't really belong to me;

and who

does

that

make

me?

So, hello there, nice to meet you.

Who am I?

I

am

no one.

The Good Old Days

As is a post-dinner tradition, the girl sits at the table, the warmth of shared memories and the late June humidity suffusing the air.

"Remember whens" and the sighs of "those were the days" linger, like the indulgence of dawdling after a meal.

And of course, there are exclamations of "kids these days," to which she rolls her eyes.

It makes her a little nervous too; what if they're right and the world is less kind to her than those that came before her? Is it ever really kind, or is it only the softness of fuzzy memory that makes the past look better?

But then again, such is life.

It's always the 'Good Old Days', but the days are never good until they're gone.

Youth (And Expectations)

They sit around the dinner table,
Reminiscing as they always do;
Those "remember whens,"
And fond sighs.

"You'll never have that."
They say.
"It all ended with us."
"Oh, what a shame."

And I smile,
I laugh at the stories,
But in the confines of my mind,
I wonder.

Are your words repeated?
Parroted generation after generation,
Because things were always better.
Simpler, nicer.

What is it about nostalgia
That colours the truth so?
Rose-tinted, stained glass.
Perfect pictures that often never existed.

And yet it's always
"Enjoy your childhood,"
The same childhood that you said
I wouldn't enjoy as you did?

Still, much of life,
Is repetition;
And I have the same laughter you did,
The same silly arguments and teasing.

It's different, of course, it is,
Worse in many ways,
But better still in others.
Just like before, just like always.

"The Good Old Days,"
But what about the
"Good Now Days,"
Forgotten and scorned?

And when those days grow old,
They'll be remembered and polished,
Rose-tinted with nostalgia,
And they'll be the new "Good Old Days."

Then again,

I am young.

What do I know of the vast ocean

Called Life?

Enough to understand that it must be cherished exactly as it is, I suppose.

Expectations (Too Many, but None at All)

The girl is thinking of the world today, and its expectations.

She supposes that the world itself doesn't want anything. It's the people in it that do.

And she supposes that they don't want anything from her personally. But they have expectations nevertheless.

To be, but not too much.

And in the right way; the way that they expect.

Nobody says it out loud (I suppose that's not really true), but one can feel it all the same.

Be (But Don't)

Grow;
Grow and grow;
But grow only if you
Grow as a seed does.
Slow,
Patient
Useful;
Something that can be celebrated,
And then too,
Only if you grow
In the right place
Or else
You'll be cut down,
Leaves falling like tears,
To be chopped up
And sold.

Flow;
Flow and flourish;
But only if you flow
As a brook does,
Cheerful and burbling.
Seldom fierce, but always moving,
For people to dip weary faces,
And drink;
But never,

Never as a river flows
Fast and "angry."
Because they'll inhibit
Too much of anything.

Bloom;
Bloom and blossom;
As a flower does,
Sweet and pretty,
With petals ever so delicate.
Beautiful, for another's sake;
But never,
Never grow thorns,
Even if they exist
To protect you.
They'll pick you anyway,
Despite their crimson blood,
Mingling with your tears;
They'll cut off the thorns.
"Beauty is pain."
But only when they can
Capture, then own the beauty.
Only if that beauty is a sort
That they can admire,
Or it's pain for naught.

Sing;
Sing and warble;

As the birds do,
But only if you have wings
To fly away
Before
They catch you,
Trap you
And
Put you
In a cage,
To sing when you're told to.

Be confident, but not too confident.
Be kind, but not too kind.
Be good, but not too good.
Be perfect, but not too perfect.

Be and be.
But don't be.
Live and live.
But don't live.

What a world of contrasts we live in;
But it doesn't matter,
Because whatever you do,
It's never enough.

Only Words

The girl feels an urgent need to do…something. Anything.

There is so much wrong with the world, yet all she does is sit there. All she can give is her words.

Words that nobody might read, that do nothing at all.

The Words That the Earth Cannot Speak
(Yet Screams Silently)

Once, I was beautiful.
In an era I cannot remember,
A past life that flashes in front of my eyes,
Tantalisingly, agonisingly.

My clear rivers,
Framing my face like
Long, curving tresses of hair;
Where are they now?

Now, they are thinning.
Tangled with rubbish,
With the waste you throw into my face;
Limp, just like my shackled limbs.

I feel your hideous, clanking pieces of metal
In my oceans,
Poisoning my blood,
And making me dizzy; making you dizzy.

I feel your rumbling vehicles
Running over my skin,
Pumping smoke
Into my lungs; into your lungs.

I feel you cutting down my trees,
With the agony of fingers being severed one by one;
But they always grow back.
And you always cut them down again.

My stomach roils with the garbage you feed me,
My lungs burn from your smoke.
My head aches from the weight of your carelessness,
And the stumps of my fingers are bleeding out.

And yet, when I protest at last,
With storms and droughts,
Heat and flames,
You ask me why I am cruel.

But it matters not,
For you are impermanent,
And I am eternal,
Unforgiving.

I will bear this agony for a while longer,
Because soon, so very soon,
You shall be gone,
And perhaps then,
My hair will flow blue once again.
My fingers will grow back.

And I will breathe freely again.

Bowstrings

She doesn't know why she is writing this. Her poetry feels pointless, a waste of time and paper. The minutes tick by on the clock.

There is too much to do, but not enough.

She is a taut bowstring, vibrating with energy. Yet, she cannot fire her arrows because they have nowhere to go. The target is too far, too distant to even see.

She doesn't even know what it looks like.

? (I'm Not Quite Sure)

If there is anyone at all,
Reading my rambles,
I haven't the faintest idea
Why.

Because I don't know
Anything about anything;
Is it my youth, or just me?
Even this, I do not know.

In truth, I am befuddled.
Perplexed
And flummoxed
By everything and everyone.

I feel as though the weeks are blowing away.
Thoughtlessly, like
Dandelions
On a stray breeze;
Everything is
Toofast toofast toofast.

Before I finish
Pondering one moment, I am
Pummelled with the next

And thenext thenext thenext
And yet another.

Before I know it,
My youth will not shield me from the world,
And I will be a child in an adult's skin;
Already, it frightens me.

Impossible Knots

Her thoughts are tangled up, like the finest thread. She tries her best to untangle them, but they snarl into an impossible knot.

What does she have left then, to make a tapestry of her mind?

Nothing.

Her loom remains empty.

Words (Or Rather the Lack of)

I
have
nothing
to
say.

The ocean of words
Inside me,
The torrents of
Stories;
Where have they gone?

That feeling of melancholy;
It, too, has disappeared,
But it has taken my words
Away with it.

Should I wish
For it back?
Wish for the melancholy to
Fill my head with
Words, words, words;
Falling from my eyes,
Rolling down my lips,
Staining pristine paper

With ink and ideas,
As teardrops
Soil pages with sorrow.

These words too,
They feel meaningless;
There is a stopper at the
Top of my heart.
There are words rushing in from below and above,
But they have nowhere to go,
Because the stopper sits stubborn,
Unknown even to me.
So, my heart swells uncomfortably,
Bursting, bursting with words.
That I do not know the shape of.

Nothing I write
Feels right,
But I have a story lodged in my throat.
Like a fishbone,
Stabbing and puncturing
Drawing blood.

I feel the pressure of it
Crushing me;
A shadow behind me,

As I go through
The motions of life.

Soon, my stoppered heart will burst.
And perhaps that story
Will be lying among the gore;
Under the mass of still-warm flesh,
Perhaps there will be a story
Too tremendous
For me to have told.

These words have not flowed
Gently, soothingly, mildly.
They have been *ripped* from my heart
Cruelly, unwillingly, viciously.
They fought and struggled
To be freed from the confines of my mind,
And trapped once again on a page.

So here lie my words,
Pickling in a pool of honey,
To sweeten their blow, their truth.
But the honey is saccharine.
And speckled with blood.

Skies and Oceans

This time, she is, indeed, staring at the sky.

She wonders what it has seen.

She wonders if it is lonely.

The ocean teases the sky, always turning the same colour as it.

But her heart aches, for she knows they can never meet.

At the same time, she feels so... small.

The world is so vast, and she is no one at all.

The Sun. The Stars (and Everything Beyond)

The sun, the stars,
The skies and everything beyond,
All eternal witnesses to
The melodrama that is mankind.

To think that we are,
But mere specks in a vast
Chasm of existence;
An abyss so deep,
We cannot fathom its size.

We think ourselves evolved,
Changed from the primitive,
But we seek still,
Exactly the same things;
Comfort, sated hunger, shelter,
Joy and all that leads us to it.

The sun, the stars, and all the rest,
How can the world be so vast?
How can it be that billions of people,
Each has a life unique to one another,
That each has their own version of the last minute,
The last hour, the last day,

All existing in the same place?

The sun, the stars, and everything beyond,
How can it be that each idea,
Has not already been thought?
That each song has not already been sung,
That each poem has not already
Been penned; yet still,
It has not.
And that, perhaps, is the beauty of humanity.

We would ruin the world,
We would tear down everything, everything in our way,
All in an attempt,
To make art,
To seek joy,
To do something not done before,
To feel a little less inconsequential,
In an existence filled with,
Stars and oceans, skies and everything beyond,
We (I) still have the audacity to believe in the ability of
humanity to create something of beauty.

Sentimentality

She is not usually sentimental.

Then again, sometimes she is. It hits her at strange times, this sentimentality.

And she feels it now as she leaves this place behind.

It doesn't tug or tear at her heart.

Instead, it merely follows her like a shadow, reminding her of what she is walking away from.

Memories (In Walls and Otherwise)

There are moments in time,
Imprinted in the fissures of these walls,
That I leave behind;
The speckles on the ceiling, a constellation of my life.

Each scrawl of pencil,
Each scab of paint
Tells a story,
If only you listen.

The stain of artistic fancies,
Painted in crimson and black
On my bedroom floor,
Still plasticky and shining.

The chip in the wall
Where I scraped the paint off,
The white dust lodged
Under my fingernails.

A corner where I stubbed a toe,
A drawer that stabbed me in the side.
Tiles that I have smashed hundreds
Of teacups on.

These walls hold memories;
Echoes of laughter and silence,
Of tottering footsteps and lengthening strides
And thus, I leave a legacy.

Save it for a Special Occasion

There is a drawer in her dresser that is saved for someday.

Sheet masks that she uses sparingly before something important.

Expensive makeup that couldn't possibly be used for just another day.

Her favourite pink pen, the one that has an ostentatiously large ball of fur with bunny ears on top: what if it runs out of ink?

The last of the yellow star-shaped beads in the box. What if she needs it tomorrow, the day after, next month?

It would be a greater shame, though, if she never used these things at all, and eventually she looked back and wondered why she ever thought these things valuable at all.

Someday (That Never Comes)

Next to her bed,
On the dark wood of the night table,
A tub of lip balm sits.
Its surface is smooth, perfectly flat,
Halfway full, but so immaculate
That it may as well have been new.

A bottle of expensive perfume
On the dressing table,
Saved for special occasions that
Come and go.
Older now, she doesn't even enjoy its scent anymore.

A box of press-on nails in
The top right drawer.
Once again, put away,
For a day more remarkable than one
Simply spent being alive.

A book that she has squirrelled away,
Something in reserve,
Something that she will pick up on her next flight,
The next weekend,
But never now.
The words in it wander into the sky,
Lost to someday.

Growing Apart

The girl blinked, and she is already sixteen.

Barely a year, and the familiar rhythm of her dearest friendship would change.

Not for the worse, she hopes, but you can never really tell with these things.

The Sacred Sisterhood of Secrets (and Memories)

For three years, we have known each other.
One where we were acquaintances,
One good friends,
And this past one, as close as close can be.

I am almost afraid to write it,
To speak it out loud,
Should the sacred sanctity of what we have,
Break and blow away with the wind,
Leaving me to grapple with the solitude I previously had,
But never realised before you.

When I think of you,
I think of staying up till 3;
Secrets wafting in the air around us,
Making us giggle, if only for the sudden
Vulnerability of words never said out loud before.

Even if, one day,
We grew apart, something I hate to think of,
I could never think of the four of us with cool distance,
dispassionate nostalgia.

Perhaps that's what everyone thinks of the friendships made in youth.

One day, you're making plans for the future and plans for today, tomorrow.

Then tomorrow comes, and if you're not in it,

Know that I wouldn't be either,

Or at least the me that I am,

Without you.

Nail Polish

She paints her nails.

Even this, she cannot do well.

The colour seeps into her cuticles, stains her clothes. It refuses to be even, and she refuses to let it remain imperfect.

The bottle is nearly empty now, but she's not finished.

Perfection (and the Impossibility of It)

My nails are painted pink;
Not like the beginning of
A blush, the tint of smiling lips.
But a pink so deep it's almost crimson.

I frown;
There is a chip in the paint
On the littlest finger
Of my right hand.

I open the squarish bottle of polish,
The smell of it
Rushing at me
All at once, familiarly unpleasant.

Once, twice
I swipe the brush
Over the chips,
To restore their perfection.

But now, it is too thick.
Clumpy and patchy,
Streaked with the precise
Lines of the brush.

The excess of pink
Runs into the crevices
Of my fingernail,
Pooling like blood.

I grimace,
Wiping the whole thing
Away with the thumb of
My left hand.

I begin again,
Painting carefully,
The lid of the bottle,
Turning pink from my stained finger.

I examine the nail,
Now perfect,
Although the skin around it,
Is smudged with pink.

I close the bottle,
Newly decorated with a fingerprint
Of pink,
My skin sticking to the fresh polish.

But I notice another chip,
This time in the nail
Of my left hand's thumb,
Where the paint peels from one side.

I open the bottle again;
Once, twice, thrice,
A million times
I repeat this charade.

Each time,
I notice a new flaw.
The blemishes double
With each second that I look at them.

The pads of my fingers,
Are sticky and pink;
The black of the brush handle
Is nearly gone.

The skin of each of my fingers
Is stained pink too.
My cuticles are red and raw from rubbing.
But it
is
still

not

perfect.

And now,

Now the air smells acrid.

Like the slow decay

Of too many expectations.

(Or just the one that matters - the expectation of perfection)

Melancholy

She is melancholy once again. Why, she does not know. In fact, mere hours ago, she could not stop smiling. She had floated, light as a bubble, far from reality.

But invisible anchors had tied themselves to her feet, and she was being pulled down.

Down, down.

Down to reality.

Joy (and Sorrow)

Why is it that sorrow lingers?
While joy is as fleeting,
And fickle
As time?

This afternoon,
I sat on a bench,
Sunlight searing my skin,
My shoes stained with mud.

My eyes were watering;
My stomach aching,
And I could not, for the life of me,
Stop laughing.

I doubled over,
Once, twice,
Shaking with
Suppressed mirth.

But now,
I feel no urge to laugh;
I cannot even
Remember the joke.

Yet, when I think of disappointments,
Of small sorrows,
They sober me instantly.
Cold water on a red ember.

Tomorrow

The girl cannot bring herself to write or draw or do anything at all today. She reads endlessly, sprawled on her bed.

She has too much to do, but she does not get up.

She has too much to do, so it's easier to do nothing at all.

Tomorrow.

Tomorrow, for certain, she will do things.

And there she lies, waiting for tomorrow, tomorrow, tomorrow.

Time (T   I   M E)

M
o
n
d
a
y
Tuesday
We dn es d ay
Thursday
Fridaysaturday
And Sun d ay.

I can't help
But measure
My life in weekends;
It is as though everything in between
Is a placeholder.

Next weekend,
For certain,
I shall do
Whatever I need to.

But my limbs are glued to the couch,
My eyes to my book;
Yet all I can think about
Is how much I have to do.

Each weekend seems
Like a reminder,
That the clock is tick-
Tickticking, tickticking.

How many more weekends
Till I do those thousand things?
The list is growing and growing.
But still, I sit,
Still, I sleep,
Still, I think.

Something Else, Somewhere Else

The heat is particularly ruthless today; it wraps around her almost tangibly.

Her head dangles off the couch as she lies upside down. She wishes it were winter already. How she hates summer.

When it is winter, she lies on the couch, armed with blankets and curses the cold. She wishes it were summer already. How she hates winter.

And so, all year long, she waits for those few days between summer and winter, and winter and summer; those few perfect days, and back to wishing for something else.

Contrasts (and Ingratitude)

I loathe summer;
The awful heat
That envelops me in
Its sweaty embrace.

But what about
Those long summer days,
Lying in the sun-warmed grass,
Laughing about everything and nothing?

Those mere minutes spent sitting on scorching steps,
Faces awash in golden light,
Burning, burning,
Yet oddly comforting?

What about
Those hours of languor,
Stretched out in
Midafternoon heat?

Sometimes,
I'm not too fond
Of winter either;
Ungrateful, I know.

But I love

Flannel blankets,

And rich hot chocolate from that one café,

And the bracing cold.

I love that

Mild winter sun,

Yellow and feeble,

The gentle caresses of warmth.

Make of that,

What you will,

Whether it spells out balance,

Or simply my disloyalty (or that of humans to extremes).

Remembering

She remembers laughing.

But already she cannot remember why, and it scares her.

If she cannot remember this now, will she remember that laughter at all in ten, twenty, thirty years?

Already, she cannot bear to lose that laughter and those that caused it; it scares her that the loss might be voluntary.

That one day, she would simply look at those numbers saved to her favourites list and find that she could not remember the last time she had called. Or been called.

And she would remove them from that list because what was the point? The list would fill with other names.

So, she would send a "Hi."

A "How are you?".

Nicknames and inside jokes, secrets and sisterhood turned into formal greetings.

She weeps already for what the future might bring.

Remember (Or Not)

I remember,
Though one memory has merged
With hundreds of others;
I remember.

I remember my fingers,
Stained orange from cheese puffs;
Your feet propped on the table,
In each other's laps.

I remember,
Our laughter,
Over what, I cannot recall
But it left us gasping.

I remember,
We were late for class,
Running up the stairs,
Wheezing and stumbling.

I remember,
Another day;
Three sitting in a row,
On a weathered wooden bench.

Summer had just begun.
It was warm,
Nearly unpleasantly so;
Nearly, but not quite.

We were languid in the sunlight,
Yet again, laughing.
Laughing so hard,
I couldn't breathe.

There again,
We were late,
And we ran across the field,
Crashing into one another, laughter making us clumsy.

I remember
For the time being;
I remember,
But for how long?

These are trivial moments;
There one second and gone the next.
How long will I remember?
Do *you* even remember?

Already I dread
The years stealing
My memories away,
Those cruel, cruel thieves.

Worse, in ten years,
Will I look back,
And cringe at this version of myself,
As I have done to my younger selves?

Will those whom I share my laughter with,
Fade away;
Eleven telephone calls a day,
Turning into a nostalgic sigh over a photograph?

One day,
I might not be the first one you tell about the most trivial
things.
I might not call you to tell you about what I ate for lunch.
What if one day I have to find that you moved to another
country through a social media post?

It has not happened yet.
Maybe, won't ever,
But already I feel my heart seizing from the grief of it.
The idea that we could be nothing but strangers with a
shared childhood.

Destiny

Already, people are asking.

What next?

What do you want to study?

What do you want to do with your life?

The girl doesn't know.

Is she supposed to know?

All of fourteen years old, and expected to decide her
destiny.

Following (But Which Path?)

Follow your heart,
They say;
All those meandering books,
Princesses and poems.

But my heart
I think
Is curiously still;
It waits, drowsy, uninterested.

My heart does not know
What it wants,
And my brain
Is aware of too much of it.

I am young, I know;
I know it's early,
But I can't help but worry,
That my heart isn't like the others.

So here I lie,
Feeling too much but little,
Thinking of everything,
But nothing.

Traps

Again, she is trapped.

Trapped not in a physical cage or a prison.

But in her mind.

She has time, but not enough; too much. The hours stretch by, but when she looks at the clock, she is perpetually surprised to find that so much of the day has gone by.

But still, she sits and she thinks. Thinks but never does. Thinks but never just *lives*.

Time (Too Much. Not Enough)

Time is such a funny thing,
Fickle and foolish,
Or maybe, it merely bears the blame
For human folly.

The TV blares behind me,
An endless cacophony;
Both comforting,
And disorienting.

The words of the book,
That I hold in my hands,
Link wondrously
Into sentences, then pages, then chapters.

And when I look up,
The sun has bid
The world farewell,
And night has fallen already.

A sudden panic seizes me;
Where
has
the

time
gone?

And it's not once,
But a million times,
That Time has stolen
Its hours from me.

But perhaps I'm
The thief;
Clutching stolen moments,
And unpaid dues.

I know I should be writing,
Studying;
Doing something *useful*,
With my time.

Five more minutes, I think.
But seven more to start
At a nice, round-numbered time.
Then again, seven's too in between.

Two minutes first,
Then five again;
A distinction
That makes sense only to me.

One

Two

That's a nice number too, but short.

Again

One

Two

Threefourfivesix.

Alas, wrong again.

What shall I do but wait four minutes more?

One, two

Threefour;

The right, round time, but a strange laziness plagues me;

Five more minutes

And then I'll study.

The end of this chapter,

And then I'll get up.

I'll do it all after dinner.

At ten, then.

Oh well, it's too late now.

Tomorrow.

For sure this time.

One day, I wonder,

Will I look up

From my book or wake
From my reveries
To find unfamiliar hands,
Wrinkled like raisins,
And dotted with age,
Palms rough and scarred.

When I clutch my face,
Will my skin sag, leathery and lined?
Eyes yellowed,
My hair more silver than brown?

And still,
Will I look back down?
And think
five
more
minutes
And then I'll deal with it?

How much will Time take?
How much time will it take?
For Time to punish
My ingratitude?

Even now,

I am stuck in an endless loop;

Five more minutes,

Then again

just

five

more

minutes

and I'll be done.

Faster. Slower. Stay

Time moves too fast, but too slow; too many contrasts.

She does not know if she wants it to go faster or slower. There are things to look forward to, but once gone, her now will never return.

Enjoying the present is something she has not quite mastered yet.

Time (Again)

Another one about time;
It beguiles me and annoys me so;
How can I be so fascinated
By something not even tangible?

I cannot fathom
That I am already
Approaching fifteen,
Edging closer to adulthood.

It feels as though
Just yesterday,
I had been eleven,
Ten, nine, wishing I were older.

I don't resent it,
But it amazes me;
Soon, in a year or a decade,
I'll marvel that I was once fourteen.

Parts and Pieces

She sits at that table where she began. The pile of paper is growing, yet she doesn't know whether to be happy.

She wonders if in a year or two she'll look back and think that she should not have written this. That she should have used a different word, or omitted it entirely.

That she will look at a poem and wonder what in the world she was thinking when she wrote it, and cringe to think that other people might have read it.

She wonders who that future version of herself is.

She wonders if those little things that make her herself will still persist. And if they won't, then who will she be?

What makes her herself after all?

Her favourite colour, her preferred music, the style of her clothes. If they change, will she lose a part of herself?

If she sheds too many pieces, will she become someone else entirely?

Wonder (Who Are You, Future Self?)

I wonder,
In a decade,
Or two or even five,
Who will I be?

I know,
It's a waste of time to wonder,
And I'll be who I'll be;
But how funny to imagine it.

Will I look back fondly
At the memory of writing this,
Lying on the couch,
Unencumbered by spellings?

If I forget, then to my future self,
Read this and remember, remember each detail of who
you were;
Remember the smell of glittery coconut lip gloss,
Of the textbook you tossed carelessly aside.

Or perhaps, will I regret it?
This and all else that
I've written, everything
I've said and done.

Will I embarrass myself in the future
As my past selves
Now do to me?
Already, I cringe.

Will those faces
That make me laugh now,
Still surround me,
Or will they be just memories?

Will my hair be short or long?
Brown or green,
Nails painted red or black,
My glasses round or square?

These little mysteries fascinate me;
Inconsequential as they are,
They will soon,
Be the fragments of my new identity.

But each "new identity,"
Is just a mishmash of the last,
And the one before;
A quilt, a thousand times redone.

Hourglasses (So Fragile)

years, years, years, years, years, years, years
days, days, days, days, days, days
seconds, seconds, seconds.
all slipping, slipping
away like

s

a

n

d

panic panic
filling me, filling me.
how many more grains are
left left left left left left left left left left
in this fragile, fragile, fragile, fragile hourglass.

Phases

It's a phase, but she should still know.

She will change her mind, but she should still know.

Too young, but old enough.

Future (Don't Ask)

F
u
t
u
r
e

I don't know what I want;
I just find it ridiculous
That I am expected,
At the ripe old age of fourteen,
To know what I wish to do
With the rest of my life.

And if I do know, after all,
Then I'm dismissed for being too young.
Because "it's a phase."
"You'll change your mind."
And "You'll grow out of it."

Sunsets

Today, she is, in fact, watching the sunset. The sky is pink, blue, and orange, and the ocean copies it shamelessly.

Waves lap at her ankles, merely a brush, yet she fears that she will be pulled in.

The sand is soft under her toes, wet and eager to take the shape of her feet.

The wind blows, and for that moment, only for that moment, she feels perfectly content.

Peace (Or Something Remarkably Like It)

I've never liked the ocean.

What scares me
It's not that it's deep, endlessly deep,
Or vaster than I could imagine,
But that it's tumultuous.

A small wave that laps at my ankles,
A tinier one that caresses my toes,
Then suddenly,
The ocean swallows me whole.

I can't see what's under it;
The things, the creatures
That live in it,
The waves that crash over me.

Will the creatures tickle
My kicking feet
To torment me,
To tell me that they lie beneath, to feast on my corpse's
flesh?

The ruthless waves,
Will they toss me
Back and forth, under and up,
Just to test my mortality?

(Perhaps I'm only being dramatic.)
Yet still
I stand
On a beach.

The sun is setting,
The sky is blue
And orange
And pink
And purple.

I can see the moon and
A solitary star,
And its dipping companion
The sun.

A crab skitters by,
And my hands
Are filled with
Broken seashells.

The wind is careless,
Blowing this way and that,
And my hair is halfway over my eyes,
Dyed blue and faded green,
Like the ocean.

And I
Am enveloped
By tranquillity,
Even faced
With my own mortality.

Stories

The girl is annoyed with herself. She thinks too much, thinks of useless things. She's too sentimental, even when she claims not to be.

For her, the skies and the oceans are lonely, the wind is playful, and all the world's in a drama.

Sometimes, sometimes, she wishes she didn't think so much. But then she thinks of her stories, and she's glad she does.

Thinking (Too Much)

Sometimes I wonder;
Why can't I just let things
Be?

Why must I think
And consider,
Deliberate,
And ponder;
Moulding my inane mental monologue
Into a saccharine song,
And then offer it to people to peruse?

But then I end up
Thinking about thinking,
Which I think
Is far less interesting.

Snarled Thoughts

Her thoughts are tangled again. She had thought that she had been doing a good job of untangling them. But now, she has reached a knot that she does not quite know how to undo. She fiddles with it, pulls at it, picks at it.

She only manages to snarl it tighter.

Emptiness (Debilitating)

The emptiness of
These endless pages
crushes
me.

Where it once
Was freeing,
An eternity of possibility,
It scares me now,
Wraps me in its blank embrace,
Chokes me with a sickening smile.
Perhaps all of my words before these,
Have been flukes, just luck and chance.

Where
have
my
words
gone?
(again)

Glances

The girl wonders how she looks to others. She wonders what they think of her at first glance.

But then she realises that they don't think of her at all.

Perception (of Others)

I wonder what people think.
Of me,
When they spare a glance.

My blue hair
Cut to my shoulders.

My pink glasses
Round as the moon

My nails
Perpetually painted, the colour always changing.

The other tiny details;
My earrings, necklace, shoes.

What do they think of me?
Who do they think I am?

Then again,
Why would they think of me?
A stranger, maybe not,
At all?

Then, I wonder
Who am I in the minds of
The people who know me?

The Mysteries of Art

She has been reading poetry. Not hers, but others'.

The poets are so unhappy; not always, but more often than not, really.

Their misery bleeds from their hearts onto paper, into her own heart.

She wonders what it is about poetry that draws the despondent.

She wonders what it is about poetry that draws *her*.

Poetry (Hearts on Paper. Broken or Not)

All these poems that I read-
Why are they so sad?
Like the fragments
Of broken hearts
Taped together
And stuck to a page.

And mine?
Mine aren't *sad,*
But there's always
That thread of melancholy
That threatens to creep in;
That always lurks
At the corners of my page.

If not sad,
Then always so
Intense,
Like the heat
And the fiery passion
Of souls bottled up
Like ink,
And spilled across pages,
Still glowing and smoking.

What is it about poetry

That demands such honesty,

Such vulnerability,

Such sadness?It is more than showing the world

Your heart.

Poetry bares the darker chambers

Of the mind

For all to see,

Draws truths from my soul.

that even I don't know of;

Each line

A discovering,

A reconciliation,

A refusal,

A question,

A demand;

An acceptance.

Nothing

Today, she is doing nothing at all. Again.

Her papers, her poetry, flutter in the wind from the ceiling fan.

Her book lies open on the table beside her, face down.

She's thinking, but of nothing in particular. She always thinks, but now she thinks inanely.

Her eyes are glued to some faraway spot as she dreams.

Yet she's not really *doing* anything.

She's only... breathing.

Existing.

Living.

A Perfect World (That Doesn't Exist)

Wasting time?
Is it even possible
To *waste* time,
As one wastes
Food or water?

Who gets to decide what
Is an 'appropriate' use of time?
Why is it that being busy with things
That don't fulfil you
Is so praiseworthy?
It's not *bad*, and sometimes it's necessary;
It's only *bad* when *idealised*.

Sitting still, doing nothing at all.
Isn't *wasting time;*
It could be gratitude,
For each moment,
Marvelling at even
The simple act of breathing.

In a perfect world,
One would have the time,
The freedom, the ability,

To read endless stacks of books,
Even if they're only picture books;
To paint,
Even if it turns out 'ugly';
To spend lazy afternoons
Doing nothing at all,
But relishing the feeling
Of being alive,
The rise and fall
Of your breath;
To spend hours lying in the grass,
Letting curious ants trace patterns
Across your skin;
Letting the wind caress you
With soothing hands.
Letting the sun warm
Your very soul.

I find it so strange
And sad
That this is considered.
A *privilege.*

Alas,
We do not live
In a perfect world,

But if doing things that
'Waste time'
Also bring you joy,
Then why should you stop?

Yet I wish
That we could all stumble and stroll
Through life,
Rather than hurry,
Hurry
To the end.

Tears of the Sky

The sky is crying.

The girl traces a stray raindrop's path as it slips down her windowpane. She wishes she could wipe the sky's tears, console it. But its tears water the earth; even in its grief, it gives and gives.

Then again, she knows that the skies don't cry.

But people do.

Empathy (The Places We Look For it)

When it rains,

Is the sky *crying*

Or do we merely

Like to believe

That we are not alone

In our sorrow?

When a river flows,

Does it *rage*

Or do we only need to know,

That there are others,

Who feel wrath and resentment as we do?

When a brook burbles,

Is it *laughing,*

Or is it just that

We need to believe

That there is reason,

Cause in the world,

To laugh freely and endlessly?

When the wind blows,

Does it *wail,*

Or do we merely want

To believe that
Another's grief can be
So profound?

Hands, but So Much More

A glance at her fingers has produced a renewed sense of wonder for the girl. Those fingers that have held and given, broken and fixed.

She marvels at them.

Hands (and Legs and Voices and Hearts)

Look at your hands,
Your fingers,
That have held others,
Brushed away tears, yours and those of others.

Your legs,
That have carried you to
Places far, far;
Leading you to your dreams.

Your voice,
That has produced music.
Words of beauty,
Of anger, of love.

Your heart, that feels.
So strongly;
That beats to
keep
you
here.

Curves and Lines and Dots

The girl is looking at her words. But she isn't writing them or reading them. Instead, she looks at the shape of them: those curves, their dashes, the dots.

How strange that they can reflect her mind, drawing truths that she is not even aware of.

Words (Most Curious)

Words are so funny;
An artful twist of the lips,
A bend of the wrist,
A few clicks,
And you have a series of words;
Words that can make people
Feel.

How strange;
These mere shapes,
These strange squiggles,
And dashes and curves.
These sounds and stops,
Gasps and pauses.
They make people laugh and cry,
Smile and frown.

How utterly bizarre
That entire stories are conveyed
Through these words;
Tales of hope and sadness,
Love and fear,
And people
Understand.

How peculiar.

Everything is All Wrong

She sits on her school bus and thinks; she's lamenting, really.

The air conditioning is too mild for this summer heat.

Her legs are too long to fit in comfortably.

The children are too noisy.

The sun is too bright, and it's shining her way.

Why won't the sunshine retreat for her?

How unreasonable of the sun.

Childhood (All Sorts)

I frown at the sun,
It shines too brightly today.
I chose the wrong side
Of the bus to sit on.

Through the blinding light,
I squint,
Down, down,
At the cars below.

Right next to my bus,
Is a child
And his mother,
In a car.

The mother holds him in her lap,
Cartoons blaring on her phone;
And yet the child kicks out a leg,
The other, and frowns.

His eyes fill with tears,
And they roll down his small face.
He wails,
Rosebud mouth twisting.

The stoplight turns green,
And we both speed away.
Opposite directions;
Away from the moment I stole.

A little farther,
And a clatter distracts me.
Across the road, a group of children
Are dragging an uprooted bathtub.

They pull on the ropes attached,
While the oldest girl gives out commands,
They push back and forth,
Until their captain is satisfied.

With her permission,
The younger ones climb in,
Packed like starving sardines,
In a dirty, cracking tub.

The others shake the tub,
Strong but still gentle,
And the children shriek with delight,
Clutching the chipped sides.

My lips twist into a smile
Without my permission.
Behind me, two children are betting
On who can hit the other the hardest.

And then there's me,
Hardly a child,
But barely not.
In between, middling.

Childhood, so different, but all the same.

Ungrateful Once Again

The girl feels... withered today.

The light seems to find unflattering angles for everyone and everything. There's colour, the world has yet to turn grey. But there's no beauty in it.

The girl sighs.

Broken (and Sometimes Reconstructed)

Sometimes, I am a house, rebuilt.
But I don't know which wicked fire burned my bones.

I am a flightless bird,
But I don't know which cruel hands tore my wings.

I am a painting, slashed.
But I don't know which sword ripped through me.

I am a song, melody stolen.
But I don't know which voice stole my music.

I,
I am a tree with no leaves,
But I don't know which storm snatched my green.

Maybe it's me.
I'm the fire.
The hands.
The sword.
The voice.
The storm.

Maybe it's me.

Untangled

The pile has grown to a stack now, and the girl doesn't know what to make of it. It's a stack of words that mean everything and nothing, a thorough dissection of who she is and what she is and who she's going to be.

At least the spool of her tangled thoughts has ended, and now her tapestry has begun.

The story inside her feels less like a fishbone and more like an idea, and she is grateful beyond belief for this.

The End (At Last)

My words have put up a fight.
But here they are at last;
Coated in honey
And needlessly sentimental,
Rambling and pointless-

But here they are.

Acknowledgements

This book was written sporadically over a year or two, sometimes typed into my phone under the haze of the late hour, a document of all my indulgent musings before it was anything else.

As always, thank you to my parents for always supporting whatever my latest interests or hobbies may be, and for believing in my writing.

To Anika, Namita, and Tara, for being part of many of the memories that I have written about, but also for being the best friends I could ask for.

And lastly, as is custom, to those who are reading this, for giving this book and the reveries of a child a chance.

9 7 9 8 8 9 7 2 4 9 4 6 6